Collins Engli

Amazing Entrepreneurs and Business People

Level 4
CEF B2

Text by
Katerina Mestheneou

Series edited by
Fiona MacKenzie

Collins

HarperCollins Publishers
77–85 Fulham Palace Road
Hammersmith London W6 8JB

10 9 8 7 6 5 4 3 2 1

Original text
© The Amazing People Club Ltd

Adapted text
© HarperCollins Publishers Ltd 2014

ISBN: 978-0-00-754511-7

Collins® is a registered trademark of
HarperCollins Publishers Limited

www.collinselt.com

A catalogue record for this book is available
from the British Library

Printed in the UK by Martins the Printers

HarperCollins does not warrant that
www.collinselt.com or any other website
mentioned in this title will be provided
uninterrupted, that any website will be
error free, that defects will be corrected, or
that the website or the server that makes it
available are free of viruses or bugs. For full
terms and conditions please refer to the site
terms provided on the website.

These readers are based on original texts
(BioViews®) published by The Amazing
People Club group.® BioViews® and The
Amazing People Club® are registered
trademarks and represent the views of the
author.

BioViews® are scripted virtual interview
based on research about a person's life and
times. As in any story, the words are only
an interpretation of what the individuals
mentioned in the BioViews® could have
said. Although the interpretations are
based on available research, they do not
purport to represent the actual views of
the people mentioned. The interpretations
are made in good faith, recognizing that
other interpretations could also be made.
The author and publisher disclaim any
responsibility from any action that readers
take regarding the BioViews® for educational
or other purposes. Any use of the BioViews®
materials is the sole responsibility of the
reader and should be supported by their own
independent research.

Cover image © Paul Brennan/Shutterstock

◆ CONTENTS ◆

◆ INTRODUCTION ◆

Collins Amazing People Readers are collections of short stories. Each book presents the life story of five or six people whose lives and achievements have made a difference to our world today. The stories are carefully graded to ensure that you, the reader, will both enjoy and benefit from your reading experience.

You can choose to enjoy the book from start to finish or to dip into your favourite story straight away. Each story is entirely independent.

After every story a short timeline brings together the most important events in each person's life into one short report. The timeline is a useful tool for revision purposes.

Words which are above the required reading level are underlined the first time they appear in each story. All underlined words are defined in the glossary at the back of the book. Levels 1 and 2 take their definitions from the *Collins COBUILD Essential English Dictionary* and levels 3 and 4 from the *Collins COBUILD Advanced English Dictionary*.

To support both teachers and learners, additional materials are available online at www.collinselt.com/readers.

The Amazing People Club®

Collins Amazing People Readers are adaptations of original texts published by The Amazing People Club. The Amazing People Club is an educational publishing house. It was founded in 2006 by educational psychologist and management leader Dr Charles Margerison and publishes books, eBooks, audio books, iBooks and video content, which bring readers 'face to face' with many of the world's most inspiring and influential characters from the fields of art, science, music, politics, medicine and business.

4

◆ THE GRADING SCHEME ◆

The Collins COBUILD Grading Scheme has been created using the most up-to-date language usage information available today. Each level is guided by a brand new comprehensive grammar and vocabulary framework, ensuring that the series will perfectly match readers' abilities.

		CEF band	Pages	Word count	Headwords
Level 1	elementary	A2	64	5,000–8,000	approx. 700
Level 2	pre-intermediate	A2–B1	80	8,000–11,000	approx. 900
Level 3	intermediate	B1	96	11,000–15,000	approx. 1,100
Level 4	upper intermediate	B2	112	15,000–19,000	approx. 1,700

For more information on the Collins COBUILD Grading Scheme, including a full list of the grammar structures found at each level, go to www.collinselt.com/readers/gradingscheme.

Also available online: Make sure that you are reading at the right level by checking your level on our website (www.collinselt.com/readers/levelcheck).

Henry J. Heinz

◆ ◆

1844–1919

the man who invented tomato ketchup

I always loved growing and selling vegetables. I worked at other professions but I always returned to my garden. I never imagined that a simple tomato sauce would have such an impact on the world.

◆ ◆ ◆

I was born on 11th October 1844, in Pittsburgh, Pennsylvania, in the USA, and I was the first of eight children. My parents named me Henry John Heinz, a name I later used for my company, H. J. Heinz. Four years before my birth, my parents had <u>emigrated</u> to the USA from Bavaria in Germany. In the beginning, life was difficult for them as they did not speak English. However, they had come to America to work hard and create a better life for themselves and their family, and that is what they did.

In 1850, we moved to a town eight kilometres from Pittsburgh called Sharpsburg. My father, John Henry, had a brickyard – a place where bricks used in construction work were made and sold. On one side of the brickyard there was some spare land that my father did not use and on it, my mother Anna Margaretha grew all of our fruit and vegetables.

I learned a great deal from my mother and father. They worked hard, saved their money and sent me to school to make sure I had a good education. When I was 14, my parents wanted me to become a priest and they even enrolled me in a special school. They were both religious people and they were members of a type of <u>Protestant</u> church. However, this was not the career I wanted to follow.

I think I had a natural talent for business because when I was 8 years old, I started selling my mother's vegetables to our neighbours. By the time I was 12, I was growing vegetables on a piece of land that measured more than 14 square metres. I had a long list of customers, some who were even as far away as Pittsburgh. Two years later, I did a couple of classes in accounting at a school called Duff's Mercantile College, which was the first business school in America.

My mother had started making different kinds of pickles. These were vegetables that had been kept in either vinegar or salt water for a few months. They developed a strong flavour from the vinegar or salt and became really tasty. I also sold these to the customers we already had, and by selling in the streets, our customer list grew.

In 1859, when I was 15, I stopped taking classes at school and went to work with my father at the brickyard. I continued growing and selling vegetables and pickles, but I also started a little business all of my own. One of the vegetables we grew was a small plant called horseradish, whose roots had a strong spicy taste. It was possible to make a white sauce from the roots, which was very good when eaten with roast beef. I started selling my horseradish sauce along with the other vegetables.

I was not the first person to sell horseradish sauce but mine was presented in a different way. Until now, all the other sellers of the sauce put it into dark glass bottles, so that you couldn't see what was inside. Some of the manufacturers had a bad reputation because pieces of other cheaper vegetables, and even small pieces of wood, had been found in their sauces. I put my sauces into transparent glass jars so the customer could see exactly what they were buying. Almost overnight, my horseradish sauce and pickles became amazingly popular.

In 1865, with the money I had made from selling horseradish sauce, and the wages I was earning, I bought half of my father's business. The population of towns like Sharpsburg and Pittsburgh was growing, and people needed new houses to live in. It was a good time to be making and selling bricks. Three years later, one of my friends called Clarence Noble also became a partner in the brickyard. It was a profitable business but I felt that for me, something was missing and I knew that I didn't want to stay at the brickyard permanently. I missed growing vegetables and making pickles and horseradish sauce, so Clarence and I went into a different business.

In 1869, we started the Anchor Pickle & Vinegar Works. In addition to our horseradish sauce, we also produced pickled cucumbers and <u>celery</u> sauce. The following year we changed the name of our company to Heinz, Noble & Company. It may sound rather impressive but in reality it was quite simple. I decided that I did not want to wait for customers to come to me. Instead, I went into the streets and sold our products from a cart that was pulled by a horse. By taking our products to the people, we got direct feedback without the need of a <u>market researcher</u> with a questionnaire. Every day, we talked with the local people. None of our customers was rich and they spent their money carefully, so it was important for me to provide quality products that were also healthy.

The other important thing I did in 1869 was to get married. My wife, Sarah Sloan Young, was also from a family of <u>immigrants</u> – hers had come to the USA from Ireland. Everyone called her Sallie. We started our family quickly, and over the next 15 years we had five children: Irene, Clarence, Howard, Robert and Clifford. Little

Robert was our fourth child, but sadly he died a month after he was born.

In 1872, my partner Clarence and I went to the Philadelphia <u>Fair</u> to present our pickles and sauces, which people seemed to like. Back home, we had also started selling sauerkraut – cabbage that had been chopped into small pieces and stored in salt – which had a delicious sour taste. Our business continued to do well until 1873, when the whole country suffered from a financial crisis that resulted in an economic depression. After the end of the <u>American Civil War</u>, the construction of the railroad – the railway system – became the second largest industry in the country. The largest was agriculture.

Between 1866 and 1873 more than 56,000 kilometres of railway track was laid across the country. A banking company called Jay Cooke and Company had invested huge amounts of money in the railroad. They had also paid for railway tracks that were going to be put on land that was not yet ready for construction. Either it still belonged to private individuals and hadn't yet been bought by the government, or the necessary preparations on the land had not been made. This meant that the company had to wait a long time before it could make any profit. Having spent all their money buying construction materials, there was no money to pay salaries and the other expenses a company has, and they started to get in debt.

It soon became impossible for them to keep the company open and on 8th September 1873, they declared that they were bankrupt – that they did not have enough money to pay their debts. Many other companies lost money, too, and also became bankrupt. In just two years, 18,000 companies closed and unemployment rose to 14 per cent. Now that so many people had no work and very little money, they stopped buying our products. In 1875, we had debts of $170,000 and we had to declare ourselves bankrupt. We had lost everything – our investment and our income – and it was a huge shock.

However, instead of allowing the situation to defeat me, I proposed a solution. On 1st January 1876, I called the members of my family to attend a meeting. I wanted to start another business but if you have declared yourself to be bankrupt, you cannot have another business in your name. I asked my brother John and our cousin Frederick and his wife two things. Firstly, I asked if they would lend me the money to start a new company and secondly, I asked if they would be the official owners. They agreed and the new company was called F. & J. Heinz. Although legally, I was the manager and not one of the owners, in reality the company was mine and I started work with a new sense of confidence and enthusiasm.

◆ ◆ ◆

A new company has to have a new product and I decided to make a tomato sauce, or ketchup, as I called it. There are two theories explaining where the name ketchup came from. The first is that the word *ke-tsiap* was used in China – by the people who spoke a type of Chinese language called Amoy – to describe the salt water that types of fish were preserved in. The second is that it came from Malaysia, where it was called *kechap*. It's likely that both stories are true. In the late

1690s, samples of the liquid arrived in England and people there soon started using it to preserve local types of fish and shellfish. They called it chatchup or catsup.

I decided to base my new tomato ketchup on old recipes that used vinegar with cooked tomatoes. Explorers in South America had brought tomatoes to Europe. Then they were brought to North America by the Europeans who came to live here, particularly the Italians who had started to use tomatoes in their cooking. In the 18th and even the early 19th centuries, people in northern Europe thought that tomatoes were poisonous. The tomato plant belonged to a group of plants called nightshade or belladonna, which, because they were poisonous, were famous for being used to commit murder. Naturally, people did not want to eat them.

However, the French found a way to make a sauce from tomatoes that people were not afraid to eat. It was very tasty but it was quite complicated to make and took a long time. I discovered that in fact I could easily make a simple tomato sauce using natural ingredients that were easy to find. There was a good supply of tomatoes and so I started production of my Tomato Ketchup. People liked it and demanded more and it became an instant success. Tomato Ketchup is still a favourite in many countries, and to this day, more of it is sold than anything else that is made by Heinz.

Soon, the company was selling so much ketchup that it started to make a profit. With the money that was coming in, we were able to add other products, like apple sauce and pepper sauce to our list and we started selling sauerkraut in metal cans. As the economy improved, sales continued to increase. As a result, we were able to put our profits back into the company and employ more people. By the time the depression caused by the financial crisis ended in 1879, we had made a profit of $15,000 and we were able to pay off some of the company's debts.

In 1886, I went on a trip to Europe with my children. I had wanted to take my wife Sallie with me but she was ill and couldn't travel. In London, I visited a shop called Fortnum & Mason that sold quality exotic food products to rich people. I managed to get an interview with the manager and was able to persuade him to try seven of my sauces and pickles. He liked them and immediately agreed to sell all seven products. We also visited Germany, where I met some of my relatives for the first time. While I was in Germany, I also visited several factories and was impressed by the way they looked after their employees. I decided that when I returned to the USA, my employees would have the same benefits as the German workers.

◆ ◆ ◆

In 1888, F. & J. Heinz was doing so much business that I was able to pay back the money I had borrowed. I was now legally allowed to own a company again and I bought out my partners – my brother and cousin – so that I was the only owner. F. & J. Heinz became H. J. Heinz and I started to expand. I built bigger and better factories in Pittsburgh and our production increased.

As company profits grew, I never forgot what my mother had taught me when I was a young boy. She always said that you should behave to other people in the way that you would like them to behave to you. I also remembered the factories I had seen in Germany that treated their employees well. In each of my factories, I employed a doctor, a nurse and a dentist to look after the workers. There were roof gardens for them to go to in their breaks. As well as wanting to provide a pleasant work environment, I also wanted to make sure that there was no dirt or disease in our factories. I gave all employees uniforms and changing rooms and showers were built for everyone to use.

New items were added constantly to our list and by 1892 there were more than 60 different H. J. Heinz products. One day while I was on a train in New York, I saw an advertisement for a shoe company that said they had '21 Styles'. I thought this was impressive and decided that we should have something similar. For no particular reason, the number 57 came into my head. I liked the look and sound of the number. I got off the train and went into a café where I sat down and thought about an advertising plan. Within a week, there were newspaper advertisements and billboard signs up with our slogan 'Heinz 57 Varieties'. It was the start of a campaign to make Heinz a name that was known to everyone.

At the 1893 World's Columbian Exposition in Chicago, we had a stall on the second floor but when it opened in May, I didn't think that enough people were coming to see us. I decided we needed an advertising trick, and I designed a little green pickle – a very small cucumber – with the Heinz name pressed onto it, made into a badge that people could wear. By the time the Exposition ended in October, we had given away more than a million pickle badges. Because of this, a newspaper started calling me *The Pickle King*. With the number 57 and a funny name, we became famous.

◆ ◆ ◆

The following year I took my family on a tour of Egypt and Europe. We were away for five months. When we returned, my wife Sallie became ill with pneumonia – a disease that affects the lungs and makes it difficult to breathe – and she died. We had been married for 25 years and it was a great shock. Although I was terribly upset, I found that work helped to make me less sad and I put all my energies into the company and our products.

In 1895, we added a product to our list – baked beans – which became very popular. Beans were a cheap type of food that were full of <u>protein</u> and we created a delicious tomato sauce to make them even better. A year later in 1896, we opened our first international office in London and introduced Heinz 57 Varieties to the British. In 1897, we developed our Cream of Tomato Soup, which, as with all of our products, was made with only natural ingredients.

◆ ◆ ◆

In my view, a business should be a community of colleagues, their families and their friends. So we invited the public to visit our factories and meet our employees. In the year 1900, we celebrated the new century in style. 20,000 people came to see how we made our products and it gave them confidence in our work. Our employees were proud to show visitors around and I, too, was proud of what we had built.

I had my own philosophy about running a business. Instead of giving orders, I asked people for their opinion. I tried to build teams because I believed that sharing led to better ideas. I encouraged new methods of production and I wasn't afraid to take a few risks. We tried to learn from mistakes and to improve what we were doing.

I thought it was vital to respect everyone who worked in the company, not just the people with important positions. This meant listening to those who did the less interesting jobs, and providing opportunities for everyone. Many of our senior people had been promoted from the most basic positions in the company. Strikes never happened at Heinz. Our employees were happy and our customers satisfied, but all around, there was another danger.

Some of our competitors did not have high standards of cleanliness and some of them faced problems when their products were <u>contaminated</u> by dirt and disease. People became ill from eating certain products and the whole industry was affected. In our factories, cleanliness had always been very important but I started campaigning for a <u>Pure Food and Drug Act</u>, which then became law in 1906.

Our efforts were recognized, not just in the USA, but overseas. It was the start of our international development. In France, I received two gold medals for our production and, in 1905, we opened our first factory in England. Once again, customers supported our products. I made sure that the English factory was managed with the same caring <u>principles</u> that I insisted on in the USA. I wanted Heinz to be a place that people wanted to come and work in and so our training and education programmes were a priority. On 14th May 1919, I died from pneumonia when I was 74 years of age. In my lifetime, we had built more than 20 factories that made Heinz products, but my company was not just about sales and profits. Its success was because of people and teamwork and I knew that my son Howard would respect what I had achieved. I was sure that he would work with my high standards and would continue to bring Heinz 57 Varieties to future generations.

The Life of Henry J. Heinz

1844   Henry John Heinz was born in Pittsburgh, Pennsylvania, USA on 11th October. His parents had emigrated to the USA from Bavaria, in 1840. His father owned a business that made bricks.

1850   The Heinz family moved to Sharpsburg.

1856   While attending Duff's Mercantile College, in Pittsburgh, Henry was also assisting his mother in making pickles. He began selling them to neighbours, along with produce from their garden.

1859   Aged 15, Henry left school and began working for his father.

1865   Henry became a partner in his father's brick business.

1868   A friend, Clarence Noble, joined Henry as a partner in the brickyard.

1869   Henry and Clarence left the brick business behind and began producing horseradish sauce in transparent glass bottles. It proved an instant success. They started a company they called Anchor Pickle & Vinegar Works.

1869   Henry married Sarah Sloan Young,
        known as 'Sallie'. They later had five
        children, although one son died as
        a baby. Clarence and Henry started
        expanding their produce to include
        pickles and sauerkraut. Henry established
        a headquarters in Sharpsburg and they
        changed their name to Heinz, Noble &
        Company.

1872   Henry and Clarence attended
        the Philadelphia Fair, where they
        introduced their sauces and pickles.

1873   The financial crisis known as 'The
        Panic of 1873' began and lasted for
        four years. Henry struggled to keep his
        company from financial ruin.

1875   The company expanded and opened
        another office in St Louis. Although
        Henry borrowed money, he was finally
        forced into declaring himself bankrupt.

1876   Henry borrowed money from his
        brother, John and his cousin, Frederick.
        He started another business, called
        F. & J. Heinz Company. They introduced
        Tomato Ketchup, which today is still the
        company's most successful product.

1877–1878   The company introduced several new
            products to their range.

1879   When the financial crisis ended, the Heinz Company began to make a profit and Henry was able to pay off many of his debts.

1886   Henry travelled to Europe and England. While in England, he visited the Fortnum & Mason grocery store, which became the first shop in England to sell Heinz products. Henry returned to the USA and started offering the benefits he had seen while he was in Germany to all his employees.

1888   Henry bought out his business partners and took full control of the company. He called it the H. J. Heinz Company.

1889–1892   New products were produced and sold.

1893   At the 1893 World's Columbian Exposition in Chicago, Henry offered customers the 'Heinz Pickle Pin', a badge which became an instant hit. Henry became known as *The Pickle King*.

1894   The Heinz family began a five-month tour of Egypt and Europe. They returned on the ship, *City of Paris*, where Henry met the author Mark Twain. In the same year, Henry's wife, Sallie, died.

1895   Heinz Baked Beans were added to the
        company's product list.

1896   Henry opened the first international
        office in London. His slogan, '57
        Varieties', was introduced to the British.

1897   Heinz Cream of Tomato Soup was
        added to their product list.

1900   The Heinz Company continued to
        grow, and offered over 200 different
        products.

1905   A factory in Peckham, England was
        opened.

1906   He led a successful campaign, in favour
        of the Pure Food and Drug Act.

1919   Henry died, aged 74, in Pittsburgh,
        Pennsylvania, USA. At the time of his
        death, the Heinz Company owned over
        20 food processing factories. Henry's
        son, Howard, became President of the
        H. J. Heinz Company.

William Lever

◆ ◆ ◆

1851–1925

the man who made millions from soap

I never had any doubts about what I wanted to do with my life. I wanted to make a soap that not only smelled good but was also cheap enough for everyone to afford.

♦ ◆ ♦

I was born in Lancashire, England, on 19th September 1851. I was the seventh of eight children, with six sisters who had been born before me and a brother called James, who was younger than me. Bolton, the town we lived in, was at the centre of the Industrial Revolution. In the late 1700s, the way of life in Britain began to change. Until then, most manufacturing had been done in people's homes using very basic machines or hand-held tools. As the steam engine developed, the first factories were opened, the railways were built and people started to live in big cities and towns where the factories and other industries were based.

In Bolton, most people worked in the factories that made things from cotton and in the coal mines. They lived in cheap basic accommodation and the air was full of <u>filthy</u> smoke that filled the lungs and made it difficult to breathe. Large families lived in very small houses, often with no bathrooms, and the most basic facilities. As a result, disease spread quickly and people often died.

From 1864 until 1867, when I was 15, I was educated at the Bolton Church Institute. This was a school for poor children in Bolton and was run by a man called James Slade – a priest in the <u>Protestant</u> Church. When I left school, I went to work for my father, James, who owned a grocery shop. Serving customers all day and listening to them talk to each other and to my father, I soon learned what they needed. As well as feeding and clothing their families, they wanted to keep them clean and healthy.

Being clean was very important, not only for health reasons, but also because people didn't want their neighbours to think they had a dirty home. Soap, therefore, was something that everybody wanted. In the past, soap had been a <u>luxury</u> that only rich people could afford. But in 1791, a Frenchman called Nicholas Leblanc, who was a chemist, discovered how to make good soap from ingredients that were not expensive. Because it was made in factories, soap was now an item that most people could afford. There was one problem, though – the soap's horrible smell.

I liked soap and I became very interested in it. I began to do little experiments to see how I could make it smell better by adding different kinds of nice-smelling oil. It was just becoming known in the medical world that if you washed your hands using soap, the spread of <u>germs</u> that caused disease, <u>infection</u> and death was reduced. This was extremely important because there were no medicines that could treat and cure most of the diseases and infections that people were dying from.

My interest in soap, however, was for different reasons. I decided that at some point in the future, I was going to make and sell soap simply because women asked for it. To me, it was a challenging business opportunity. In 1872, another opportunity happened when my father made me a partner in his business. I was 21 years old. Two years later, on 15th April 1874, I got married. My wife was called Elizabeth Ellen Hulme and we had known each other since early childhood. Her family lived in the same street as mine and we had gone to the same school.

In the early years of my marriage, I worked as a travelling salesman for the family business, visiting towns in my local area and selling groceries to other shops. Each day was a chance to do real market research with shop owners and their customers, who told me what they wanted. After a while, though, I became bored with the grocery business. I had never lost my interest in soap and so I decided to start a business selling the soap that was already being made. However, I soon discovered that my customers wanted soap of a higher quality than was available.

By 1883, the solution seemed simple – I would make my own soap, which I would then sell and distribute to other shops. I was lucky because I had help. My wife played an important role in developing the business and my father promised to invest an amount of money. I had read a book – *Self Help* – written by a man called Samuel Smiles, which gave me some excellent ideas and the courage to start my own business. In 1885, my brother James also decided to come into business with me. We called the company Lever Brothers.

We did not waste any time. We rented an old soap factory, owned by a family called Winser. Percy Winser was a chemist and he joined us as an employee. By paying a very good salary, I also succeeded in getting a man called Ed Wainwright to come and work with us. Ed was not a chemist and in fact had no scientific training at all but he was a professional 'soap-boiler' – someone who makes soap – and was extremely good at his job.

With this team, I started making soap. Until that time, the main ingredient of soap was a substance called tallow. This was a hard fat that came from cows and sheep. It was also used to make candles. A local chemist called William Hough Watson invented a new way of making soap, replacing tallow with vegetable oils such as <u>palm oil</u>. Using all of our combined knowledge, we produced our first soap, which was called Honey Soap. Later called Sunlight Soap, it was mainly used for <u>household</u> tasks like washing clothes and cleaning floors. It was far better than any other soap that was being made, and within two years, production had increased so much that we needed a bigger factory.

With my profits and the money that my father had invested and lent me, I was able to raise £27,000. This was enough to buy some land where I could build my own factory. In the county of Cheshire, I bought 56 <u>acres</u> of land at a very good price. The land was cheap because most people thought it was useless. It was marshland – land that is full of water because it's near the sea – and needed to be <u>drained</u> before

it could be used for anything. This was a big and expensive job. Many people said it was risky and that I would lose my investment. They were wrong.

I called my land Port Sunlight and on 3rd March 1888, we started the building project with a big ceremony to celebrate. My intention was not just to build a factory. I wanted to build a whole village where all the employees of Lever Brothers could live happily and well. I remembered the horrible <u>over-crowded</u> living conditions in my home town, Bolton, and I did not want my employees to have the same experience.

An architect called William Owen designed the village for me, based on my own ideas and plans. We began by building 28 cottages. Each cottage had running water and an indoor bathroom – something that was quite rare for workers' houses. In addition to the land I already had, I bought another 165 acres and was able to expand and create the village of my dreams. I employed a total of 30 architects on the village, which we finished in 1914. Houses were built in small groups, and each group was designed by a different architect. In total, 700 homes were built along with schools, shops, a big church, a hospital and many sports facilities including an outdoor swimming pool. There was even a theatre.

I paid my workers a good wage, a fifth of which they had to pay back in rent. People could work, live and play in the village without ever needing to leave, but I encouraged them to travel and arranged for a railway track to be built, linking the village to the rest of the rail network. In addition to providing pleasant living conditions for my employees and their families, I wanted to make sure they were looked after financially. I paid them when they were sick and couldn't work and I also gave them a pension when their working days were over.

Also in 1888, I moved with my wife Elizabeth to a village called Thornton Hough where, in the same year, our son William was born. By this time we were producing more than 450 tons – 457,200 kilos – of Sunlight Soap every week. In 1893, I bought Thornton Manor, a big old house in Thornton, for us to live in. Then I bought the rest of the buildings in the village and with the help of several architects, transformed it into what I hoped was a perfect village.

◆ ◆ ◆

In 1894, Lever Brothers developed a soap that people could use to wash themselves with. The main ingredient was a substance called carbolic acid. This was an <u>antiseptic</u>

that doctors had been using in hospitals. Our chemists found a way to put it into our soap. The product was called Lifebuoy. As with Sunlight, it was an immediate success. By the following year, 1895, we were producing more than 400,000 kilos of the soap per year.

For the next few years I focused on advertising and marketing and I found that designing the campaigns to sell Sunlight and Lifebuoy was exciting. I wanted to expand Lever Brothers abroad and so I started travelling to faraway places, one of them being the USA. In 1898, I bought a small soap factory in Cambridge, Massachusetts.

In 1900, I visited West Africa because the palm oil we were using came from plantations owned by British companies there. By 1911, we were using far more palm oil than was available and I decided it was a sensible business decision for us to start growing our own palms. I started looking for a place to build a plantation and decided that the Belgian Congo was suitable. We created a plantation which I called Leverville to supply us with all the palm oil we needed. My goal was to make life better for the people who worked at Leverville, but local politics prevented me from doing so.

◆ ◆ ◆

In the meantime, I was also busy at home. In 1899, I bought two more properties – an estate in Horwich called Rockhaven and another one called Rivington – both near my home town, Bolton. In 1902, I joined the Freemasons. This was a very old secret society, a kind of club, for men. Members had to have strong moral beliefs and they met several times a year. Each branch of the Freemasons was called a lodge and I was the first member to have a lodge named after him.

In 1906, the other major manufacturer of soap, Joseph Watson, and I tried to create a soap <u>monopoly</u>. We wanted to get together with a few other producers of soap to stop anyone else from making and selling it. A national newspaper found out about the plans and tried to stop us by asking its readers not to buy our products. They were successful and we lost a great deal of money. We abandoned our plans, but I estimated that Lever Brothers lost about half a million pounds.

◆ ◆ ◆

My political <u>principles</u> were important to me, and I had always supported the <u>Liberal Party</u>. In 1906, I was asked if I wanted to be a candidate in the national elections for my local area, the Wirral. I was elected and became a <u>Member of Parliament</u> (MP). One of the things I campaigned for – successfully – was the introduction of a pension for people who had retired. This was similar to the one I paid my employees. The pension was first paid to people over the age of 70 in 1908.

I was still running Lever Brothers, and having a career in politics at the same time proved to be quite difficult. I stopped being an MP after three years and concentrated fully on my business. By now, the running of the company was my responsibility alone. My brother's health had always been bad and there had been periods of time, some of them lasting for a while, when he had been unable to work. In 1911, I became a <u>baronet</u>. In Britain, the king or queen has the ability to make an ordinary person, like myself, part of the <u>aristocracy</u> by giving them what is called a title. These people are chosen because they have done important work or have acted in a special way, like helping poor or sick people. There are many titles which range in importance, and it is possible for someone to be given a higher title later in life – similar to being promoted at work. Baronet is the 'lowest' title. Being a baronet also meant that I now had a place in the <u>House of Lords</u>, even though I had stopped being an MP. This way I stayed involved in politics.

Seven years before, in 1904, I had bought a house, called The Hill, in an area of London called Hampstead. The property next door – Heath Lodge – was now for sale and I bought it so that I could demolish it and make the garden at The Hill much bigger. I didn't go and live at The Hill until 1919, and then I spent most of my time there.

Then dark days came. In 1913, my wife died, which was a terrible sadness and a year later, the <u>First World War</u> started. Many men from our village volunteered to join the army and the local branch of the army, the Wirral <u>Battalion</u>, mainly consisted of Lever Brothers employees. Sadness and depression soon filled the factory and our village as families learned of the terrible news from the war.

Almost every family had a son, father, husband or brother who was either wounded or killed. Four hundred local men died. By the end of the war in 1918, more than 900,000 British soldiers had been killed and another two million had been wounded. Naturally, it was hard to keep the business going without men to work, so I started to employ women. After the war, we wanted to show our respect for the local men who had died. I paid for a war <u>memorial</u> to be built in the village for the soldiers and sailors. Above the list of names was written: THESE ARE NOT DEAD — SUCH SPIRITS NEVER DIE.

In 1917, I bought an island called Lewis, which was part of a group of islands off the coast of western Scotland called the Outer Hebrides. I developed a company called MacFisheries and tried to provide more secure work for local people. However, not everyone there wanted to move into the industrial world. A better standard of living did not always mean a better standard of life. In 1923, understanding why the local people did not want to change their traditional way of life, I offered to give the Isle of Lewis to its inhabitants, but they refused. In the end I sold the land to someone else.

Also in 1917, before the end of the war, my title of Baronet was changed to that of <u>Baron</u>. I added my wife's name to my own and I became Lord Leverhulme. The link between

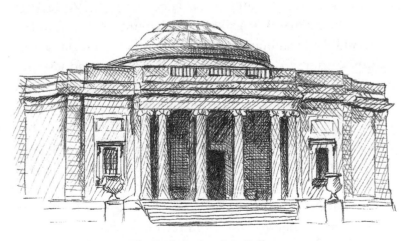

The Lady Lever Art Gallery

politics and business had always been important to me and in 1918, when the people of Bolton asked me to become its mayor, I accepted. It was an honour for me and I wanted to serve the people of my home town.

In 1922, my title was changed again and I became a <u>viscount</u>. In the same year, I opened an art gallery in memory of my wife. I had been collecting paintings for quite a while and wanted the gallery to be a memorial to Elizabeth and her achievements. The Lady Lever Art Gallery was built in a beautiful garden in Port Sunlight, not far from where we had put the war memorial.

◆ ◆ ◆

In my later years I was able to provide money for different kinds of research. The Liverpool School of Tropical Medicine was established and I created the Leverhulme Trust to help with the publication of research and medical works. In 1925, I became ill with the disease pneumonia and on 7th May, I died at my home in Hampstead in London. I felt that my purpose in life was to introduce new ideas and to create a better working world. I wanted a place where we worked to live, not lived to work, and I think I managed this at Port Sunlight.

All the money I made had been earned from the manufacture and sale of soap. It was earned by the employees of Lever Brothers, which has now become the international company, Unilever. Port Sunlight is also still there, after 100 and more years. It is a fine example of what people can achieve when they work together.

The Life of William Lever

1851   William was born in Bolton, Lancashire, England. He was the seventh of eight children.

1864–1867   William was educated at Bolton Church Institute.

1867   He began working in the family grocery business.

1872   His father made him a partner in the family business.

1874   William married Elizabeth Hulme.

1880   He learned about the importance of soap while working as a travelling salesman for his father's business.

1883   William developed plans for a new business in the soap-manufacturing industry.

1885   He established Lever Brothers, a soap-manufacturing company, with his brother, James.

1887   He bought 56 acres of land on the Wirral in Cheshire, which became known as Port Sunlight.

1888   Work began on the Port Sunlight village.
        It was developed as a place for Lever
        Brothers's employees to live. William and
        Elizabeth moved to Thornton Hough.
        Their son, William Hulme Lever was born.

1889   The painting, *The New Frock*, by William
        Powell Frith, was bought to promote his
        company's product, Sunlight Soap.

1893   He bought Thornton Manor and then the
        village of Thornton.

1894   Lever Brothers started selling Lifebuoy soap.

1898   The company bought the first soap-
        manufacturing factory in the United
        States. It was a small factory in Cambridge,
        Massachusetts.

1899   William bought the state of Rockhaven in
        Horwich. A year later he also bought the
        Rivington Estate.

1900   He got his supply of palm oil from the
        colonies in British West Africa.

1902   William became a member of the
        Freemasons and was the first to have a
        lodge with his name – William Hesketh
        Lever Lodge No. 2916.

1904   William bought his London home, The Hill, at Hampstead.

1906   He was unsuccessful in his attempt to establish a soap monopoly with several other large manufacturers. He built Saint George's United Reformed Church. William became the MP for the Wirral area until 1909.

1911   William bought Heath Lodge – the property next door to The Hill in London – which he demolished to extend his garden. He became a baronet. He also visited the Belgian Congo for supplies of palm oil.

1913   His wife, Elizabeth, died.

1917   William was given the title of Baron Leverhulme and also High Sheriff of Lancashire. He visited, and then bought, the Isle of Lewis in the Outer Hebrides.

1918   The citizens of Bolton invited William to become Mayor of Bolton.

1919   William moved to The Hill and spent most of his time there. He bought an estate on the island of Harris in the Outer Hebrides. A town was later named Leverburgh.

1922   He built the Lady Lever Art Gallery.
        William was given the title of Viscount
        Leverhulme.

1925   William died, aged 73, at his home in
        Hampstead. His funeral was attended by
        30,000 people.

Michael Marks

◆ ◆ ◆

1859–1907

founder of the Marks & Spencer stores

My success was built on three things: hard work, the determination to succeed and the will to live. Without them I know I would not have survived. However, I cannot ignore the important role that a single penny also played.

◆ ◆ ◆

I was born in 1859 in the city of Slonim, a <u>province</u> in Russia that is now called Belarus. I was the youngest of five children. I never knew my mother, Rachael, because she died a short time after my birth. My father, Mordechai, had to bring up his children without their mother. Fortunately my elder sister was old enough to help him look after us. It was a difficult time for us because we were <u>Jewish</u>. There had always been a great deal of discrimination against <u>Jews</u> throughout the Russian <u>Empire</u> and it was hard to make a living. There were many violent attacks – called *pogroms* in the Yiddish language – on Jewish businesses and individuals.

As a teenager, I quickly realized that there was no future for me in Slonim. My brothers and sisters had grown up and were living their own lives, but I wanted to find a better place with more opportunities. I decided to look for a new life, but I didn't know where I would find it.

In 1880, my family wished me well, and waved goodbye to me for the last time. At the age of 21, determined to succeed, I started the long walk across Europe. The first thousand miles were the worst. I walked from village to village, and town to town, trying to find temporary jobs. Communication was difficult as I heard languages that were strange and new to me. I did not know what was ahead, but I managed to survive.

♦ ◆ ♦

The days turned into weeks and then months as I travelled across Poland, Germany, and France. Whenever I could, I worked to earn enough money to buy food and I slept wherever I could find a suitable place to lie down. I realized it was not easy to make friends. Some people were kind, but most did not want to know me. I was a foreigner who did not speak their language. I was dressed in poor clothes that certainly did not improve in appearance as my journey went on.

Along the way, I heard there were many Jews in England and it became my dream to go there. It was nearly two years before I reached the French coast. Then I travelled across the sea in an old boat that looked as if it might sink. When I arrived in my new home, it did not feel like home at all. There were no family or friends to greet me, as I had none.

There was no job waiting for me, as I had no trade and I could not even speak English. The worst thing, though, was that I did not have any money.

When I arrived in London in 1882, I met some Jewish people who understood my language. That was one piece of good luck, but it wasn't enough as they had no work for me. I really thought I might <u>starve</u>. Then someone told me to travel north and go to the city of Leeds in Yorkshire. Apparently, there was a company there called Barran's that made clothes in a factory. They told me that Barran's employed a lot of <u>immigrants</u>, especially Jews, so I decided to go there.

As I had no money to take the train, I had to walk. It was another long walk of over 300 kilometres in the rain and wind. Arriving in Leeds, a busy noisy city, I must have looked a terrible mess – dirty and rough from my journey. When I tried to speak, people walked past, not understanding me. After a while I found someone who understood the one word I said – 'Barran's' – and he showed me the way.

◆ ◆ ◆

In 1884, I met two well-dressed men, one of whom could speak some Yiddish. The other one, whose name was Isaac Dewhirst, had a business selling good quality but inexpensive <u>household</u> items. I explained who I was and where I had come from and Isaac Dewhirst invited me to his warehouse – the place where he kept his products. There, I met other men who spoke Yiddish and I described my journey from Slonim. Mr Dewhirst listened while someone translated my story. I explained about the *pogroms* and the way I had escaped from a difficult and possibly dangerous life, and about the journey I had taken across Europe.

Clearly, Mr Dewhirst was impressed that I had survived. I think he also saw my determination to succeed because he offered me five pounds, which was an enormous amount of money at the time. It was also a considerable risk for him as he did not know me or what kind of person I was. I was very grateful for his offer but I turned it down. I didn't want money, I wanted an opportunity to get into business. I asked him if instead of the money, I could have some of his products to sell. He agreed and we selected which items I should take.

I started visiting the small villages and towns near Leeds where I sold the goods. As soon as I had sold everything, I returned to Mr Dewhirst with the money I had made. He was pleased to see me and gave me more of his products. I returned to the places I had been to before, as well as going to new villages and towns.

Gradually, I became a familiar face and as people started to trust me, they bought my products. Although I was learning basic English, I still found the language quite difficult. I had a sign made that said, 'Don't Ask the Price, It's a Penny', which made things easier. Although people were buying my products and I was making money, the time I spent travelling from place to place reduced the amount of time I had for selling the products. It was time to take the next step.

With the money I had saved, I set up a stall in the market in Leeds that was held each Tuesday and Saturday. I also had stalls in markets that were held in the towns of Wakefield and Castleford. Once again, I put a sign on my stall that said, quite simply, 'It's a Penny'. People liked that, and they supported my business.

On the days I wasn't at any of the markets, I travelled, and one day I went to a place called Stockton-on-Tees, which was about 100 kilometres from Leeds. It started to rain heavily, and while I was inside keeping dry, I got into conversation with a man called Mr Cohen. I recognized his accent and I mentioned that I came from Slonim. He told me he was a refugee from Russia, and invited me to his home. He had a beautiful daughter called Hannah who was about the same age as I was, and I was made welcome in their home. Meeting Hannah was a turning point in my life.

Within a year, on 19th November 1886, we got married. Sadly, our first son, who was born in 1887, died during the birth but fortunately we were able to have two more children, Simon who was born in 1888 and then Rebecca. Hannah helped me with the business, preparing the stock for sale and dealing with the finances.

◆ ◆ ◆

The business continued to grow, and in 1891, we decided to move from Leeds to a town called Wigan in Lancashire, about 90 kilometres away from Leeds. It was a smaller town than Leeds, but we had a bigger house. Moving also enabled me to expand the business into Lancashire and Cheshire, where I set up more stalls in the indoor markets of various towns. Indoor markets were developed in the 19th century. Often, they were built especially, and in some towns famous architects were employed to design big, impressive buildings. They protected shoppers and sellers from the weather. They were also safer than being in the street. By 1894, my business had grown so much that I realized I needed a partner who could focus more on the paperwork in the office, while I continued to concentrate on sales.

On a visit to Leeds one day, I asked Mr Dewhirst if he was interested in working with me as a partner. He was still my main supplier of household products and we had a good working relationship. This time he declined my request but he suggested that I asked a man called Thomas Spencer, who worked in his office. Thomas was interested and agreed to buy 50 per cent of my business for £300. We started our business with five words in our minds: quality, value, service, innovation and trust. On 28th September 1894, when Marks & Spencer officially started as a company, we had no idea that it would become so hugely famous.

Thomas Spencer bought 50 per cent of Marks' business in 1894

We combined our talents. I was responsible for selling and marketing and Thomas focused on finance and distribution issues. Thomas was very practical and due to his years working for Dewhirst, he knew many people and was able to get us goods at the best prices. My job was also to find new markets and organize the sales teams. Soon we had many market stalls in different towns and cities such as Manchester, Birmingham, Bristol, Cardiff, Hull, Liverpool, Middlesbrough, Sheffield and Sunderland. It was a good partnership and business increased.

In 1897, I was proud to become a British citizen. This country had given me a new start in life. We called our new stalls Penny Bazaars and added a sign saying 'Admission Free'. This meant that people could come in and just look around without having to buy anything, which at that time, was unusual. We sold biscuits, wool for mending clothes, pins and needles, combs and socks. We also sold sheet music so that people could play popular music and songs on their own musical instruments.

By 1900, we had a total of 36 Penny Bazaars, and shops in the high streets of 12 towns and cities. The following year, we built our first warehouse in Manchester and this became our company headquarters. By 1903, Marks & Spencer had become a public company and our investment was now valued at £15,000. Now that we were listed in the Stock Market, we could raise more capital to expand.

In 1905, at the age of 53, Tom Spencer retired and sadly, in the summer of the same year, he died. A man called William Chapman represented the Spencer family in the business after Thomas's death. I invited a man called

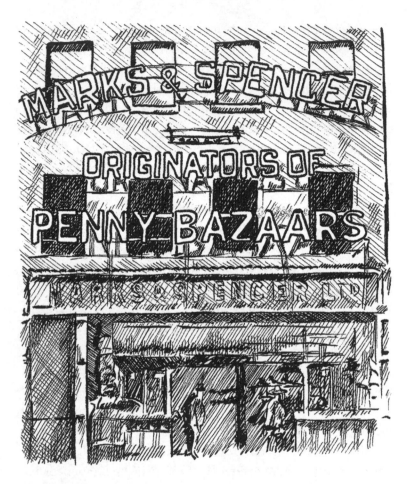

Bernhard Steel to join us, and he represented my family, and we also employed new and younger managers. We now had a major shop in London, and seven branches.

I could hardly believe that I had managed to get the new life I had been searching for. Despite having had no training, I built a very successful business. I started with nothing, but worked hard and gained valuable experience.

In this new world of mine I was able to provide a far better future for my family than I had ever dreamed was possible.

However, on 31st December 1907, I collapsed and died, aged 48. I did not know it, but Marks & Spencer continued on into the future. After my death, my son Simon took over the business and had a major influence on its development. There are now Marks & Spencer's shops in more than 40 countries all over the world.

The Life of Michael Marks

1859 Michael Marks was born in Slonim, a
      province in Russia that is now called
      Belarus. He was the youngest of five
      children.

1880 Aged 21, Michael left home and made his
      way to Europe.

1882 He <u>immigrated</u> to England and then moved
      to Leeds, seeking employment.

1884 Michael met Isaac Dewhirst, the owner of
      a Leeds warehouse. He began successfully
      selling Isaac's goods in nearby villages.
      He set up a stall in Leeds Market and sold
      quality small goods for one penny. He
      used the <u>slogan</u>, 'Don't Ask the Price, It's
      a Penny'.

1886 Michael married Hannah Cohen in Leeds.
      They later had a son, Simon, followed by a
      daughter, Rebecca.

1891 Michael moved his family to the town
      of Wigan.

1894 He asked Isaac Dewhirst to become a
partner in business. Isaac declined the
offer, but suggested that an employee of
his, Thomas Spencer, might be interested.
Thomas agreed and they formed Marks
& Spencer. They opened market stalls
in Manchester, Birmingham, Liverpool,
Middlesbrough, Sheffield, Bristol, Hull,
Sunderland and Cardiff.

1897 Michael became a British citizen.

1901 The first Marks & Spencer warehouse in
Manchester was built. They already had
36 stalls, including seven in London and
Bradford, Leicester, Northampton, Preston
and Swansea.

1903 Marks & Spencer became a public company.

1905 Thomas Spencer retired and was replaced
by William Chapman.

1907 Michael died aged 48. His son, Simon,
continued to run a number of his father's
'Penny Bazaars', which he turned into
a major British chain with shops in
40 countries.

Henry Ford

◆ ◆ ◆

1863–1947

the man who mass-produced cars and made
them affordable

I always loved engines and machines of all kinds. I liked steam engines, and I was happy when cars were invented, but I was delighted when I was able to make cars available to everyone.

◆ ◆ ◆

I was born on a farm in Greenfield Township, Michigan, USA on 30th July 1863. I always said it would have been more appropriate if I had been born in a factory, as that is where I spent most of my life. My father, William, was born in Ireland, but came to America as an <u>immigrant</u>, like hundreds of thousands of other Irish people in the 1840s. The reason for this was the Great Potato <u>Famine</u>. The potato was one of the basic foods in Ireland but in the summer of 1845, something went wrong and the crop failed. The potatoes grew normally without problems, but when they were taken from the ground, they started to go black and rotten.

The cause was discovered to be a type of <u>fungus</u> that had come to Ireland from Mexico. Potatoes had been grown because just one <u>acre</u> of land could produce enough of them to feed a large family for a whole year. Without potatoes there was nothing to eat and people <u>starved</u> or died from what they called Famine Fever. This was not one disease, but several terrible diseases like cholera, dysentery or typhus. A quarter of a million people died in the following ten years and another two million, like my father, left their homes and went to Britain, Canada or the USA.

My father came to Michigan, where he met my mother. Her name was Mary Litogot and they got married and set up a small farm. They had me first and then my four other brothers and sisters were born, but sadly, my mother died in 1876, when I was 13 years old. She had taught me to read and helped me develop <u>self-discipline</u> and I missed her.

We went to school but educational facilities were limited to the one-room school that our village had. I had always been interested in how machines worked. When I was about 13, my father gave me a watch. The first thing I did was to take it to pieces to see how it worked and fortunately, I was able to put it together again afterwards. In 1879, when I was 16, I decided I needed to find work and be independent. I could have worked on my father's farm but I didn't really enjoy farm life. One day I left the farm and walked the 14.5 kilometres to the city of Detroit.

First, I worked for the Michigan Car Company, which gave me a clear understanding of how cars were built. Then, I got an <u>apprenticeship</u> working with different kinds of machines. I worked first with James F. Flower &

Brothers, where I stayed for two years and then I moved to the Detroit Dry Dock Company. From the first day, I knew my future was with machines, not animals. I also knew that machines would one day <u>revolutionize</u> farming.

In 1882, I went back home to the farm. To help my father with some of the work, we got a Westinghouse Farm Engine, which used steam to power it. I still didn't much like farming. Instead I was employed by Westinghouse to look after and clean the steam engines that other farmers in our area were using. At the same time, I studied accounting at college. My social life was also busy as I enjoyed dancing, and ice skating on our frozen lakes in winter.

The Westinghouse Farm Engine

One day I met a young woman called Clara Bryant. We liked spending time together and in 1888, we got married. I earned a living by farming and also by running a sawmill – a factory where wood is cut into long thin pieces. It was also a time when I had lots of ideas about machines and I would often bring engines or parts of engines home, where somehow they always ended up spread all over the house. This was fun, but I needed work that was more challenging and the chance to turn some of my ideas into reality. To do that I also needed time and money.

In 1891, the Edison Illuminating Company offered me a job as an engineer and so we moved to Detroit. I didn't know much about electricity but I quickly learned. Two years later in 1893, I became the organization's Chief Engineer. Now that I had a steady job and money coming in regularly, I was able to continue developing my ideas by experimenting. One of these experiments was to make a petrol–powered car. This work was done at home at weekends and in the evenings. I was not the only person who spent his free time trying to invent a car that did not need to be pulled by horses. It was like a race to see who would invent one first. My life was already becoming very interesting and when our son, Edsel, was born, I considered 1893 to be a fortunate year for me.

By 1896, the Ford Quadricycle, as I called it, was ready to drive and I did my first test drive on 4th June. It had two <u>cylinders</u>, a steel frame and four bicycle tyres but I soon realized that I needed to do some more work on it. While I was working on the second model, I met Thomas Edison, whose company I was employed by. He encouraged me to continue with my improvements and in 1898 a new model was ready to be launched. Making the Quadricycle, however, was expensive and I spent time looking for people who would invest in its production. A man called William H. Murphy, who had the biggest wood business in Detroit, agreed to support me. I resigned from Edison's and in August 1899, I set up my own business which I called the Detroit Automobile Company.

However, I didn't know very much about running a company and after a short time, I was having to deal with various problems to do with the quality and pricing of my automobiles, as cars were called then. I decided to sell the company and invest the money I had made in new ideas. At this time, I was a racing driver and had won some important races, driving a car that I had designed and built myself.

Potential new business partners had seen me racing, and some of them wanted to invest in my 26-horsepower vehicle. With their financial help, I set up a second business in 1901 called the Henry Ford Company. I had the title of Chief Engineer. The following year, however, I had a serious disagreement with my investors when they brought in an outside consultant called Henry M. Leyland. This was the man who designed a car called the Cadillac. I left the company and without me, they called it the Cadillac Automobile Company, which later became a major competitor of mine.

In 1903, at the age of 40, I felt it was time to focus seriously on my business, so I started a new organization called the Ford Motor Company which immediately started producing cars. I knew that the future for transport on land was on the roads. The railways were expanding rapidly, but only from town to town. A car, however, could go anywhere and everywhere once roads were built, but people were still mainly using the horse and cart. I realized there could be a mass market for cars.

Within just a few weeks of starting business, our first Model A cars had been sold, and in less than a year, 859 cars had been bought. The Model A was an 8-horsepower engine with two cylinders, which could reach a speed of 48 kilometres an hour. It became known as the Fordmobile.

In 1904, we needed a larger space to work, and we built a plant – that's what the car factories were called – in a place called Piquette Avenue. New investors, the Malcolmson Group, supported me and over the next few years, we made constant improvements. By 1907, our Model N car was the best-selling car in the country and we had also started selling cars in Canada and England.

In 1908, I developed the Model T car. This could be used on the farm as well as on the road and like the Model A, was an immediate success. We were making cars as fast as we could sell them, but I wanted to be able to make them even faster and to make far more of them. At that time, each car was built by hand. The car stayed in the same place until it was finished. Each worker had to come to where the car was to do their part of the construction and it took many hours of skilled work for each car to be built. Making cars by hand was expensive and I knew there was a better way that would reduce our production costs. I just hadn't found it yet. We also needed more space.

The Model T car

In 1907, I bought 60 acres of land in a place called Highland Park, just outside Detroit, where I had a large factory built. I wanted it to be the best and most efficient car factory that had ever been made and I employed both architects and company engineers to make sure we got the design right. The main architect was a man called Albert Kahn, who later became known as one of the best industrial architects. Building the plant took two years because I wanted to use the profits we were making for the building costs and not to borrow money. Highland Park in the USA opened on 1st January 1910 and then the following year, production started in Britain.

For several years we had been looking at ways to rearrange the men and the machinery to move away from the old slow methods of production. By 1913, we had started using assembly line production. This meant that the workers stayed in one place and the car was moved along on a moving platform. Each worker completed a small task and then the car moved on to the next person. The production time of each car was reduced from 14 hours to 90 minutes. I felt we had achieved something amazing and at the same time we had created a great deal of new employment in the Detroit area.

However, the new way of working was boring and not very satisfying for the workers and they soon started to complain. In fact, many of them left. There was work for 14,000 men but in one year we had 53,000 workers passing through Highland Park. I realized I had to do something to make the job more attractive. In 1914, I introduced the five-dollars-a-day wage. This was about twice the average paid elsewhere, but paying more worked and employees now wanted to work at the Ford Motor Company.

◆ ◆ ◆

In 1914, far away in Europe, the <u>First World War</u> had begun. As we learned of the death and destruction I decided I had to try to do something to make peace. I had met a Hungarian woman called Rosika Schwimmer who was a well-known pacifist – someone who believes that violence and war is wrong. She asked me if I would pay the expenses for an expedition to Europe. The plan was to meet in a neutral country – Norway was selected – where leaders of countries not involved in the war could discuss ways of stopping it.

On 4th December, we set off for Europe with more than 100 other pacifists on a ship called *The Oscar II*. I had discussed the expedition with the American President, Mr Wilson, to see if we could get approval and support from the government, but he refused. Our trip and the meetings that followed were unsuccessful and I returned, disappointed and upset, to the USA. Our intentions had been good but most people thought we were foolish, and that the expedition had been a complete waste of time and money. The war continued for another three years.

◆ ◆ ◆

I decided to focus on making cars and developing my business. In 1915, I bought the land for the Rouge River plant in Dearborn, Michigan and building work began two years later. Now, everything we needed to make cars could be brought to us by ship as well as by rail. I had bought a huge area of land so that we could expand without having to move again. There was enough space not only to make cars but also to make all the parts that the cars themselves were made of. We were able to make our own steel, and from raw rubber that was shipped in, we made all our own tyres.

In the meantime, my grandson Henry Ford II was born in September 1917. It was a great day and the start of a new generation. The following year, encouraged by President Wilson, I decided to enter politics and become a candidate for Senator of Michigan in the elections. I was not successful but enough people had voted for me to stop me looking ridiculous. In the same year, I bought a local newspaper called The Dearborn Independent.

In 1919, some of my investors thought that I was taking a big risk by building the Rouge River plant, and 'doing too much in one place' and they started causing trouble for me. By this time, one in every two cars made was from my factories and I was making a considerable profit. I decided that I did not have to listen to the investors any more and I bought their <u>shares</u>. This made me the only owner of the world's largest automobile company. I gave my son, Edsel, the title of Company President but in reality, I was in charge. By 1920, the first parts of the Rouge River plant were in production and I was employing more than 80,000 workers.

By 1921, we had produced our five-millionth car and by 1924, we had made ten million. We were changing the face of America, socially and economically. More people were free to travel and when in 1925, the price of a car fell to $260, the average American could afford to buy one. I was convinced that our Model T was the car that people wanted.

However, more expensive cars like the Chevrolet, which was more stylish and came in different colours, were becoming popular. Something I said once about the Model T had become famous. 'You can have any colour you like as long as it's black.' My son and other senior employees began to warn me that it was time we started making a new type of car. I didn't want to listen to them but when sales of the Model T started to fall, I had no choice.

Production of the Model T ended and we started work on a new car, which we called Model A, not to be confused with our very first Model A car. To produce the new car, we had to upgrade our machinery which meant closing for six months, causing difficulties for our employees who had no job or income during that time. Model A was launched towards the end of 1927 and on reopening, we were producing 10,000 cars a day.

The Stock Market Crash in 1929 and the economic depression that followed naturally also had an effect on the Ford Motor Company. I was forced to lower wages and reduce the amount of employees I had. I had always been against workers' unions as I saw them as just interfering in my business, but I made an effort to motivate my workers by reducing the working day from nine hours to eight. However, in 1938, I had to sign an agreement with a workers' union.

In the meantime, we continued to expand internationally and were now making vehicles in the UK, France, India, Holland and Germany. In 1938, I was presented with a medal called the Grand Cross of the German Eagle for my efforts to make motor cars available to everyone. This was the highest medal given by Nazi Germany to foreigners. Although a similar medal was also given to the Vice President of General Motors, it caused several problems for me as some people said that I supported the Germans against the Jews.

In 1941, the USA entered the Second World War when the Japanese attacked Pearl Harbor. Despite the fact that I was against any kind of war, we started making military equipment. Previously, in 1925, I had bought a business called the Stout Metal Airplane Company, and we developed an aeroplane called the Tri-Motor. Unfortunately the plane did not sell well and I had to close that part of my company. However, in 1942, we started making B-24 bomber planes and produced more than 8,000 of them. As soon as the USA became involved in the war, I put all my energies into doing whatever I could to help and I believe that we made a great contribution to our armies and our nation.

While we were busy with the war, my only son died of cancer in 1943. His death greatly affected my family and our company. By the end of the war, I was unwell – I had already had a stroke in 1938 when I was 75 years old. After my son's death, I had to take over many areas of the company he had been responsible for. Now I was quite weak and I agreed to let my grandson take over as President of the Ford Motor Company.

Two years later I died at the age of 83 at my home in Dearborn. Looking back, I had created, with the help of many, the Ford organization. It was a great company. It provided work and an income for thousands of employees. It had transformed travel for ordinary people and had raised the standard of living for their families. I considered myself to be part of a revolution that crossed the bridge from farm work to factory work, from the village to the city. The company had created a new mobile society and had set new standards in business and management throughout the world.

The Life of Henry Ford

1863   Henry was born on 30th July at the family
farm in Greenfield Township, Michigan,
USA. He was the first of five children.

1876   When Henry was 13, his mother died.

1879   Henry left home and worked for a short
time as an apprentice for the Michigan Car
Company in Detroit. He then worked with
James F. Flower & Brothers. Two years later, he
worked for the Detroit Dry Dock Company.

1882   Henry returned home to work on the family
farm where a Westinghouse steam engine
was used. The Westinghouse Company hired
him to look after the steam engines other
people had. He began studying accounting
at Goldsmith, Bryant & Stratton Business
College.

1888   Henry married Clara Bryant. He farmed 80
acres of land and ran a sawmill.

1891   He became an engineer for the Edison
Illuminating Company in Detroit.

1893   Henry's son, Edsel Ford was born. Henry
was promoted to Chief Engineer for the
Edison Illuminating Company. He began
experimenting with a petrol engine.

1896   On 4th June, Henry test drove his vehicle which he named the Ford Quadricycle.

1898   His second vehicle was completed.

1899   Henry started the Detroit Automobile Company on 5th August, with the financial backing of William H. Murphy.

1901   Detroit Automobile Company was closed. Henry designed, built and raced a 26-horsepower automobile with the help of C. Harold Wills. The Henry Ford Company was formed on 30th November, with Henry as the Chief Engineer.

1902   Henry left the company and it was renamed the Cadillac Automobile Company.

1903   The Ford Motor Company was established. The first Model A car was introduced in Detroit.

1908   Manufacturing began on the Model T car.

1910   Highland Park factory began production in Michigan.

1911   Henry opened Ford factories in Britain and Canada.

1913   Mass production on the assembly line began at Highland Park.

1914   Henry introduced the five-dollars-a-day wage.

1914   *The Oscar II*, Henry's 'Peace Ship', sailed to Norway on an expedition to end the First World War.

1917   Construction began on a new factory on the Rouge River in Dearborn, Michigan.

1918   Henry wasn't chosen as the Senator for Michigan in the elections. He bought the weekly newspaper, *The Dearborn Independent*.

1919   His son, Edsel Ford, was named President of the Ford Motor Company.

1921   The Ford Motor Company had 55 per cent of the automobile industry's total production.

1922   Henry bought the Lincoln Motor Company.

1925   He bought the Stout Metal Airplane Company.

1926   The Tri-Motor airplane and a new car, the Model A, were developed.

1927   Production of the Model T ended, and production of the Model A began at Rouge River.

1928   Henry was awarded the Franklin Institute's Elliott Cresson Medal.

1929   The New York Stock Market crashed. The world economic depression created major problems for Henry's organization.

1932   He built the first V-8 Ford Car.

1933   The Ford Airplane Division closed due to
poor sales.

1938   Ford Motor Company signed a contract with
a worker's union.

1938   Henry was presented with the Grand Cross of
the German Eagle.

1941   The USA entered the Second World War
and Henry's organization began to produce
military equipment.

1942   During the Second World War, Henry
produced around 8,000 B-24 bomber planes,
at the Willow Run manufacturing plant.

1943   Henry's son, Edsel, died.

1945   Due to Henry's ill health, his grandson, Henry
Ford II, took over the role of President of the
Ford Motor Company.

1947   Henry died, aged 83, at his home in Dearborn,
Michigan.

Coco Chanel

◆ ◆

1883–1971

the businesswoman who changed fashion
for women

I spent my life making women look and feel beautiful.
I started designing hats, moving onto sportswear and
then elegant clothes that were comfortable to wear. I also
created the magical perfume, Chanel N° 5, that made
women feel and smell gorgeous.

◆ ◆ ◆

I was born on 19th August 1883, in a place called Saumur in
western France. My parents gave me the first name Gabrielle
but I am known as Coco. My surname was Chanel and I saw
no reason to ever change it, although my birth certificate
says Chasnel, due to the bad eyesight of the person who
filled it in.

   I was born in a poorhouse run by <u>Catholic</u> <u>nuns</u>, which
as the name suggests, was a place where people could go to
sleep and eat if they had no money and nowhere to stay. My
father, Albert, was a travelling salesman who never had any
money and my mother, Jeanne, washed laundry. I was the

second of six children, although one of my brothers died when he was just a baby, and we all lived in small, noisy accommodation. We were poor and life was not easy.

One terrible day in 1895, when I was 12 years old, my mother died of a disease called bronchitis. She was 31 years old. My father could not cope with five small children. He sent my two brothers to work on a farm and took me and my sisters, Julia-Berthe and Antoinette, to a <u>convent</u> in Aubazine in central France. I never saw my father again.

We had nowhere else to go and no way of looking after ourselves. Fortunately, the nuns at the convent agreed to let us stay. They were strict, but we survived because of their care. We were given a basic education. In addition, we were taught how to be seamstresses – how to sew and make clothes. I was lucky that I had the chance to be educated and learn a useful trade. The nuns also taught us practical skills, like cooking. We were expected to pray and lead a religious life. It was a quiet, private place and we were protected from the rough life we had been born into. We only saw life outside the convent during school holidays when we visited relatives, who were kind to us.

In 1901, when I was 18 years old, I left the convent and went to stay in a Catholic <u>boarding house</u> in the town of Moulins. My first job was in a tailor's shop. It was there that I discovered I had a talent for designing hats. My hats caught the attention of ladies in the town who asked me to make more and I was able to earn extra money. It was my first step towards financial independence.

Then I met a young man called Étienne Balsan. His family were wealthy and he did not need to work so he spent his life having fun. He had wonderful manners and with him I learned how a girl from a poor background could live a life of <u>luxury</u>. He introduced me to literature, music and good food. It was impossible for a man from his rich background to marry a poor girl like me, but he became a lifelong friend.

In 1905, in addition to my work in the tailor's shop, I also started singing, working in cafés and late-night bars. Someone said that I should have a stage name so I chose Coco and I used it for the three years that I sang professionally. I soon realized that I did not have a good enough voice to make any money from singing but I kept the name Coco. It suited me and I left the name Gabrielle behind me for many years. I was ashamed of my background and I never told anyone the truth about how my father had abandoned us. Instead I made up stories and I often said that he had gone to America to look for work.

♦ ◆ ♦

In 1908, I moved to Paris where I continued designing hats. Étienne introduced me to a rich English friend of his. His name was Arthur Capel, but everyone called him Boy and he was an officer – a captain – in the British army. We became close and our friendship lasted for ten years. In the cafés where we often met, I liked sharing my ideas on designing and making hats with Boy and Étienne. Étienne was always enthusiastic and encouraging about my designs but Boy was helpful in a more practical way. He decided to invest some of his money in me and my designs and I was able to set up my own business.

In 1910, I opened my first shop, at 21, Rue Cambon, Paris, selling the hats I was designing. Although I knew little about marketing, I called the shop *Chanel Modes*. The hats that I created were worn by famous French actresses who provided me with a great deal of free advertising. Pictures of them wearing my hats appeared in magazines and as a consequence more women wanted to buy their own hats from me, and my business grew quickly. It was an exciting time and the days passed by quickly.

◆ ◆ ◆

In 1913, I opened a shop in Deauville on the north-west coast of France, also using the money that Boy had lent me. At that time there were strict rules about the kind of

clothes and styles that women could wear. The clothes were beautiful to look at but they were uncomfortable, long and tight, preventing women from moving freely. I myself had started to dress differently. I shortened the length of my dresses so my ankles showed and started to wear looser, more comfortable clothes. I made most of my clothes myself and used a material called jersey that was soft and simple. Many women asked me where I had found my dresses, skirts, jackets and tops, and I understood that there was a demand I could not ignore.

In the Deauville shop I introduced a collection of women's sportswear that looked stylish and sophisticated but was also comfortable and easy to move around in. I felt that I was responsible for changing the way women saw their bodies. I felt like I had started a revolution. The sportswear was an instant success and I became quite rich.

In 1914, the First World War began. It ruined France and the lives of the French people defending it. The fighting against the Germans was fierce and millions were killed. I concentrated on designing more clothes for women.

The relaxed, comfortable appearance of my clothes attracted younger women and in 1915, I opened my third shop, in Biarritz on the south-west coast of France. In addition to my sportswear, I started designing evening dresses. These too were popular and by the following year I was making so much money that I was able to repay Boy all of the money he had lent me. Sadly, Boy was killed in a car crash in 1918. His death had a terrible effect on me and I never really recovered from it.

In 1921, I introduced my perfume, Chanel N° 5. It was created by a man called Ernest Beaux, who had created perfumes for the Russian <u>aristocracy</u>. It was called N° 5 because it was the fifth perfume I had sampled and liked. Over the next few years I launched several other perfumes: N° 22, Gardenia, Bois Des Iles, and Cuir De Russie, but it was N° 5 that by 1929 had become the most popular perfume in the world. It also made a lot of money for me.

◆ ◆ ◆

Many people thought that I should get married but I didn't want to stop doing what I loved – helping women to look their best – and so I remained single. In fact, I thought it was my responsibility to help women look beautiful and confident. Designing clothes and running the business was exciting. In 1925, I was invited to design stage costumes for the performance of the play *Antigone*, written by a man called Jean Cocteau.

Then one day in 1926, when I was at the opera, I looked round at all the women there and was <u>horrified</u> by what I saw. They were all wearing dresses in very bright colours that I thought were really quite bad taste. I made the decision at that moment that my next designs would be in black. In those days, you only wore black if someone close to you had died or if you were a servant. I was about to change that. Once again I caused a mini-revolution when I introduced my Little Black Dress, or 'LBD' as it was later known. This was a simple, very sophisticated black dress, which was also comfortable to wear. The 'LBD' is still a fashion 'must' for women.

In 1929, I opened another shop. However, the <u>Stock Market Crash</u> of 1929 reduced people's incomes and they stopped buying luxury products like the ones I was selling. It was not a financial disaster for me, but the business took time to recover during the 1930s.

In 1931, I was invited to Hollywood to design clothes for the films produced by Samuel Goldwyn. He offered to pay me a million dollars if I came to Hollywood twice a year. I accepted his offer but my designs were not popular because they were too plain and simple. I did not like the whole scene in Hollywood. I left California and spent some more time travelling, looking for inspiration for new ideas, and I displayed my new designs in Paris.

The *House of Chanel* in Rue Cambon became well-known and in 1932, we showed a collection of beautiful diamond jewellery. The number of staff we were employing continued to grow and by 1935, there were more than 4,000 people working at Chanel. It had become a substantial business and more of my time was spent organizing than designing. My social life consisted of a continual circle of meetings and dinner parties. In 1939, just when we thought the business was secure again, the <u>Second World War</u> began and the Germans invaded.

Once more, France was nearly destroyed. Businesses closed, families were torn apart and lives were ruined. I felt it was time to stop working and I closed the shops, although I continued to live in Paris, at the Ritz Hotel. It was a tough and difficult time and nobody knew what was going to happen in the future. In 1945, I went to live in Switzerland. In the beginning I stopped working but after a while, I decided that retirement was too boring and I continued working on my designs.

In 1953, I returned to Paris and made a dramatic <u>comeback</u>. Once again, I made my home at the Ritz Hotel, which was a very expensive way to live, but I felt secure and happy there. In 1954, when I was 71, I held a fashion show to present my new designs. The French press hated my clothes and thought that at 71, I was ridiculous. However, in America, *Life* magazine loved what they saw on the <u>catwalk</u> and wrote that I had brought a revolution to the fashion world. My designs were again leading the way.

More women were entering business and needed new fashions and Chanel became a name that stood for quality and elegance. It had become fashionable again for women to wear uncomfortable clothes that required them to have tiny waists. I had always been against artificial silhouettes for women. So I designed a jacket that helped make the Coco Chanel brand name stronger than ever before. My jacket was so successful because its design was very simple. Like the skirt of the suit, it was cut straight so that it was neither too tight nor too loose, allowing women complete freedom of movement. Every woman in the public eye had a Chanel jacket.

In 1957, we won the Neiman Marcus Fashion Award. As I had no family, my work was everything to me. It gave me a purpose in life, as well as fame and fortune. I believe it was what kept me alive. In 1969, a musical was made about my life that starred Katharine Hepburn, and in 1970, aged 87, I launched our N° 19 perfume. By the following year, I had lived a full and exciting life and I died on January 10th at my home. I had already designed my own gravestone.

The Life of Coco Chanel

1883   Coco was born on 19th August in Saumur, France. Her parents named her Gabrielle Bonheur Chanel.

1895   When Coco was 12 years old, her mother died. Her father sent Coco and her sisters to a convent in Aubazine, Corrèze, France. It was there that she learned how to sew. Her two brothers were sent to work on a farm.

1901   She went to live in a Catholic boarding house in Moulins, France.

1905–1908   After leaving school, she worked in shops and sang in nightclubs. She also worked in the French resort of Vichy. When performance work as a singer was hard to find, she moved back to Moulins. She met Étienne Balsan.

1908   Coco moved to Paris and began designing hats. Étienne introduced her to Englishman, Captain Arthur Edward 'Boy' Capel.

1910   Boy Capel helped finance her first independent shop – Chanel Modes.

1913   Coco opened a second shop, also financed by Boy Capel, in Deauville.

1915–1916	Coco's third shop opened in Biarritz, on the French coast. She created unique women's evening dresses. By 1916, her success had increased and she was able to repay the loan she received from Boy Capel.
1918	Boy Capel died in a car accident and Coco never quite recovered from his death.
1921	Aged 38, she introduced her famous perfume, Chanel N° 5. It was launched two years later
1926	She introduced the 'Little Black Dress'.
1929–1930	Coco opened another shop. Chanel N° 5 became the most popular perfume in the world.
1931	She met Samuel Goldwyn, who offered her a one-million-dollar contract to design clothes for Hollywood films.
1935	Coco's business was expanding and there were 4,000 employees.
1939	When the Second World War began, Coco closed her shops. She went to live at the Ritz Hotel.
1945	After the war, she moved to Switzerland.
1953–1954	She returned to Paris and made a successful comeback.

1957 Coco received the Neiman Marcus Fashion
      Award.

1969 The musical *Coco*, based on her life,
      opened in New York, and starred Katharine
      Hepburn.

1971 Coco died aged 87, in Paris, France.

Ray Kroc

◆ ◆ ◆

1902–1984

the man who created the McDonald's chain
of restaurants

**As a young man, I met two brothers called Richard
and Maurice McDonald, who ran a small hamburger
restaurant. I didn't know then that the result would be the
chain of restaurants with the famous 'Golden Arches'.**

◆ ◆ ◆

I was born on 5ᵗʰ October 1902, in Oak Park, which was
near the city of Chicago, USA. My parents, Louis and Rose,
were of Czech origin and like all <u>immigrants</u> they worked
hard to establish a new life. Being born in America, I had
different life expectations from my parents, but I was not
afraid of hard work. Even at a young age I wanted to work
and make money, but it was a long time before I managed to
achieve my aim.

I went to school locally but I preferred action to academic
study. I left school as soon as I could and then had to decide
what job I was going to do. I could have been a professional
piano player as I had had lessons when I was younger, but I

decided I could probably earn more by going into the world of business.

In 1914, when I was 12 years old, the First World War started and the USA sent soldiers to Europe to fight the Germans. Three years later, I was still too young to fight in the military, but I lied about my age and joined the Red Cross. They were training ambulance drivers to help injured soldiers, and at my age, I saw it as an exciting opportunity. The war ended just as I was finishing my training and I wasn't sent over to Europe.

After the war ended, I did a variety of jobs, like selling lemonade and working in shops and restaurants. I learned a lot from them but I realized that I had to find work that was more serious. In 1922, I married at the age of 20, and my wife, whose name was Ethel Fleming, wanted more financial security than my jobs provided. I found work with a company called Lily Cups that sold paper cups. I discovered that I was quite a good salesman. During the day I sold cups and in the evenings I played the piano for a radio station. After a while, I left Lily Cups and started selling property in Florida. I found the work easy and I was quite good at that, too.

◆ ◆ ◆

Aged 25, I returned to Chicago, and my wife and I started a family with the first of our four children. Now it was essential for me to have a steady job with a good income and I was pleased when Lily Cups offered me a job again. The fast-food restaurants of the time were the stalls that sold food on the streets. They were good customers as they needed the paper cups I was selling. In 1929, Lily went into business with

Tulip Cups and I had a wider range of products to sell. New clients were appearing, such as <u>drugstores</u> and baseball parks. I loved the sport of baseball and Wrigley Field in Chicago – the home of the Chicago Cubs – was one of my customers. I offered advice on how to increase the number of spectators coming to watch baseball games by suggesting they sold <u>carry-out</u> food as well as drinks on the <u>stands</u>. This would also increase my sales, but the manager wasn't interested in my ideas. One of my other clients, however, was interested.

A drugstore called Walgreen Drugs tested my idea for a carry-out food service. They had already been selling to about 100 customers an hour, but I showed them how they could increase that using my products. Disposable cups and cartons cost more, but the income from using them was greater. Soon, all of their stores had carry-out food and I became a top salesman.

However, it was hard to make sales elsewhere. The <u>Stock Market Crash</u> of 1929 had ruined many businesses and had led to the 1930s being years of serious economic depression. They were also the years of <u>Prohibition</u>. In 1925, the production of alcohol was banned in the USA, which meant that people started spending money on soft drinks. This led to the development of dairy bars – these were places that sold soft drinks. One of my clients, Ralph Sullivan, reduced costs with a new product made from milk and ice cream called a milkshake. He was very successful. Realizing this was an opportunity for me to make some money, I took his idea to a man called Earl Prince. He owned ice cream parlours – a type of café that sold ice cream – and he agreed to try selling milkshakes. Milkshakes were so popular that

Earl Prince needed more cups than he usually ordered. He became my best customer and bought five million cups a year.

We talked about the plans that he had to further improve his business. He was a mechanical engineer and had developed a new machine which made milkshakes faster than someone could make them by hand. He called it a 'Multimixer' and I thought it was a real <u>innovation</u>. I showed it to managers at Lily-Tulip to see if they were interested in distributing it to their clients. To my complete amazement, they turned the idea down. It was an opportunity that I could not miss, but would I be able to run my own business successfully?

It was 1939, and I was 37 years old. I decided to take a risk. Earl Prince agreed to give me the marketing rights to the Multimixer. I set up a company to sell the Multimixer, which I called Malt-A-Mixer Company. My clients were people who owned <u>soda fountains</u>, bars and restaurants and used the Multimixer to make all kinds of drinks. We changed our name to Prince Castle Sales and we were doing well, but then, in 1941, the Japanese bombed <u>Pearl Harbor</u> and the USA entered the <u>Second World War</u>. We had to stop production of the Multimixer because supplies of the metal we used to make it were no longer available.

◆ ◆ ◆

To make an income during the war, I worked with a man called Harry Burke. He had a product that gave ice cream a sweeter taste. Added to the frozen milk that was used to make milkshakes, it was a cheaper version of ice cream and it helped our organization to survive the war years. After the war, we were able to sell the Multimixer again. It was popular, and we sold 9,000 units a year.

By the late 1940s, my income had risen to $25,000 a year, which was a great deal of money in those days. However, in the 1950s, we were faced with competition from other companies which reduced our own sales. In addition, the soda fountains, which bought two-thirds of the Multimixers that were sold, were slowly becoming fewer in number. We looked for new products to sell, but could not find anything that we thought would be successful.

◆ ◆ ◆

The McDonald organization in San Bernardino, California, was one of my existing customers. In 1954, when they ordered their eighth Multimixer, I decided to visit and see what they were doing with all those drink mixers. It was a long and expensive flight to California, but it changed my life because what I found out surprised me. The McDonald brothers were not in the soft drink business, they were fast-food operators, selling hamburgers. They had bought the Multimixers because so many of their customers wanted a milkshake with their meal.

This made me think about my business strategy. Should I be trying to sell more products to the fast-food operators? Or perhaps I should invest in an opportunity that was just opening up with the McDonald brothers? They had a small franchise operation with eight branches and the agent who managed the branches for them was leaving. With my sales skills, I could make the franchise larger and could make a great deal of money.

The brothers agreed but had several conditions. They limited the cost of buying into the franchise to $950, which I thought was a small amount of money. The percentage that I got from sales was 1.4, which was an even smaller amount. Looking back, it was not a good deal and I was never going to make enough of a profit. However, at the time, I did not know that.

I had also thought that I was going to make money by selling Multimixers. Then I realized that most <u>franchisees</u> would only buy two mixers and that each one usually lasted for ten years before it needed to be replaced. I kept thinking, trying to find a business idea that would be successful.

With the franchise operation, we had only considered expanding in California, in addition to the eight branches the brothers had already <u>franchised</u>. I thought that we should consider expanding to include the whole country. After all, people ate a lot of hamburgers. The McDonalds agreed to the idea if I managed it, and on 2nd March 1955, we formed McDonald's Systems Incorporated. In the same year, our first restaurant was opened in Des Plaines, Illinois.

My approach to franchising was different to that of the brothers. The production of the hamburgers and the way they were served stayed the same, but I wanted to make other changes. I wanted to make it easier for the franchisees to succeed. I thought it was wrong to make them pay all of the franchise fee before they had even started. I also wanted to provide a marketing service and support them in other ways.

It was my job to persuade people that buying a franchise was a good idea. I did so using my best selling techniques. I went from town to town, giving speech after speech to the groups of people I had to convince. There were the people who were buying the new franchises, the people who were going to lend them the money to do so, and our suppliers.

I was very grateful for my communication skills because without them I don't know if I would have succeeded. In my speeches, I focused on product, quality and cleanliness. I said how important it was to make the restaurants family-friendly and for the employees and owners to have a pleasant environment and good working conditions.

People commented on how kind they thought I was being and I told them that it was important that those involved knew I cared about them. We were all in the business together and my view was that I would only succeed if they succeeded. Keeping everything going at times was very difficult, especially as I was not very well and suffered from several serious health problems.

◆ ◆ ◆

The McDonald brothers did not want us to open so many branches and we often had disagreements. By 1961, I decided I didn't want to argue any more and I bought the brothers' shares in the company. I paid them $2.7 million. I also opened the Hamburger University. This was a training school – it still exists today – that was responsible for teaching McDonald's employees about service, quality and cleanliness. Since it opened, more than 80,000 managers and owners have attended classes. That year was quite eventful and it was also the year that my marriage ended.

◆ ◆ ◆

The 1960s were an important decade for me, both professionally and in my personal life. By 1963, I had opened our 500th restaurant, in Toledo, Ohio and I got married again, to a woman called Jane Dobbins Green. In the next two years, we opened another 200 restaurants and in 1965, McDonald's became the first fast-food company to be listed on the <u>Stock Exchange</u>. The value of the shares started at $22 each and climbed quickly to $49. By the end of the 1960s we had over 1,500 restaurants.

Over the years, I realized that the real heart of the business were the buildings themselves that the restaurants were in, as they were a <u>capital asset</u>. We were in the property business, not just the food business and that is where I really made my money.

For the restaurants, I focused on providing clean eating-places for people of all ages. Prices were low, you didn't need to make a reservation, and there was a fixed menu that did not change. The staff were trained to be polite, and customers learned to trust our quick, friendly service. Young people could get a job, an income and work experience. All of our working procedures were <u>standardized</u> to ensure efficiency, and we produced a 75-page manual for franchisees that explained everything in detail.

In 1967, we opened McDonald's restaurants in Canada and Europe and later also in South America and Asia. My business model worked in all those places and we opened restaurants in 118 countries. The restaurants served well over 50 million customers every day and McDonald's had become an international <u>household</u> word. It was not only one of the major <u>brands</u>. It was also one of the largest organizations in the world that actually owned the buildings that its branches were in. All this success proved difficult in my personal life and in 1968, my second marriage ended.

◆ ◆ ◆

I was President, then Chairman, of the organization from 1955 to 1977. I then became Senior Chairman for my remaining years. In addition, I became the owner of the San Diego Padres baseball team, but that is a different story, and in 1969, I married a woman called Joan Mansfield.

The McDonald's Corporation was more than business to me. It was a way of life and a chance to help others in need. We made large contributions to various charities, and then in 1974, we started the Ronald McDonald House. This was an organization that provided support for parents of children who were ill.

People sometimes asked me how I had managed to become so successful. Life presented me with a big opportunity that I was fortunate enough to recognize when it appeared. My life ended in 1984, when I was 81 years old. Most people knew the name McDonald's but few customers had heard of my name, Ray Kroc. I didn't mind, though, because for me, success was always a team effort.

The Life of Ray Kroc

1902   Ray was born on 5th October in Oak Park, Illinois, USA. His parents named him Raymond Albert Kroc.

1917   During the First World War, at the age of 15, Ray lied about his age and joined the Red Cross as an ambulance driver. The war ended, just as he completed his training.

1919   For the next twenty years, he worked in a wide variety of jobs. They included: working as a musician; as a radio DJ; working in a restaurant in exchange for a room and his food; and as a salesman.

1922   Ray married Ethel Fleming.

1939   He obtained the marketing rights to Multimixer and set up the Malt-A-Mixer Company. He later changed the name to Prince Castle Sales.

1954   He received an order of eight Multimixers from the McDonald Brothers. The opportunity to work as their franchising agent was offered to him.

1955   McDonald's Systems Incorporated was formed. The first McDonald's Restaurant was opened in Des Plaines, Illinois.

1961   He bought the company from the McDonald brothers for $2.7 million. Ray opened Hamburger University. In the same year, his marriage to his wife Ethel ended.

1963   Ray opened the 500th McDonald's Restaurant. He married Jane Dobbins Green.

1967   McDonald's opened in Canada and Europe.

1968   His second marriage ended.

1969   Ray married Joan Mansfield.

1974   Ronald McDonald House was established. It was an organization to support children who were ill and their families. He bought a baseball team, the San Diego Padres.

1978   The 5,000th McDonald's restaurant was opened in Japan.

1984   Ray died, aged 81, on 14th January in San Diego, California, USA. The organization called Ronald McDonald Children's Charities was founded.

acre COUNTABLE NOUN
An **acre** is a unit of area equal to 4,840 square yards or approximately 4,047 square metres.

American Civil War PROPER NOUN
The **American Civil War** was a war which took place from 1861 to 1865 between the northern and southern states of the USA. As a result of the war, slavery was abolished and the states came back together as one country.

antiseptic VARIABLE NOUN
An **antiseptic** is a substance that kills harmful bacteria.

apprenticeship VARIABLE NOUN
A young person who has an **apprenticeship** works for a fixed period of time for someone who teaches them a particular skill.

aristocracy COUNTABLE NOUN
The **aristocracy** is a class of people in some countries who have a high social rank and special titles such as Duke or Count.

baron COUNTABLE NOUN, TITLE NOUN
In Britain, a **baron** is a man who has been given the title 'Lord' by the king or queen. In the past, all barons were members of the House of Lords.

baronet COUNTABLE NOUN
In Britain, a **baronet** is a man who has been given the title 'Sir' by the king or queen, or who has the title because his father had it before him. In the past, baronets were members of the House of Lords.

battalion COUNTABLE NOUN
A **battalion** is a large group of soldiers who work together and have a lieutenant-colonel as their chief.

billboard COUNTABLE NOUN
A **billboard** is a very large board on which posters and advertisements are displayed on the street.

boarding house COUNTABLE NOUN
A **boarding house** is a house which people pay to live in.

bomber COUNTABLE NOUN
A **bomber** is a military aeroplane that drops bombs.

brand COUNTABLE NOUN
A **brand** is the name of a particular company and the

things that it sells, especially when it is very famous and has a strong reputation.

capital asset COUNTABLE NOUN
Capital assets are the things such as buildings and factory equipment that a company owns.

carry-out ADJECTIVE
In American English, **carry-out** food is hot cooked food that you buy from a shop or restaurant and eat somewhere else. The usual British word is **takeaway**.

Catholic ADJECTIVE
Catholic people and institutions belong to the Catholic Church, the branch of the Christian Church that accepts the Pope as its leader.

catwalk COUNTABLE NOUN
At a fashion show, the **catwalk** is a narrow platform that models walk along to display clothes.

celery UNCOUNTABLE NOUN
Celery is a vegetable with long pale green stalks.

charity COUNTABLE NOUN
A **charity** is an organization which raises money to help people who are ill, disabled, or poor.

comeback COUNTABLE NOUN
If someone makes a **comeback**, they return to their profession after a period away.

contaminate TRANSITIVE VERB
If food **is contaminated**, it becomes unhealthy or poisonous because germs or other bad things get into it.

convent COUNTABLE NOUN
A **convent** is a building in which a community of nuns live, often one where they have very little contact with the world outside.

cylinder COUNTABLE NOUN
In an engine, a **cylinder** is a sort of tube inside which a metal disc slides up and down to make parts of the engine move.

dark ADJECTIVE
Dark times are very sad because horrible things happen.

demand TRANSITIVE VERB
In business, if you say that people **demand** something, you mean a lot of people want it and ask to be able to buy it.
UNCOUNTABLE NOUN
If there is **demand for** something, a lot of people want it and ask to be able to buy it.

distribution VARIABLE NOUN
In business, **distribution** is the process of sending products to all the places where they will be sold.

drain TRANSITIVE VERB
If an area of land **is drained**, all the water there is made to flow somewhere else permanently so that the land can be used.

drugstore COUNTABLE NOUN
In the USA, a **drugstore** is a shop where drugs and medicines are sold, and where you can buy make-up, some household goods, and also drinks and snacks.

emigrate INTRANSITIVE VERB
If you **emigrate**, you leave your own country to go and live in another.

empire COUNTABLE NOUN
An **empire** is a group of countries controlled by one powerful country.

fair COUNTABLE NOUN
A **fair** is a big event at which companies display or sell goods, and which has visitors from a long way away as well as from the local area.

famine VARIABLE NOUN
A **famine** is a time when there is a serious shortage of food in a country, which may cause many deaths.

fast food UNCOUNTABLE NOUN
Fast food is hot food such as hamburgers which is served quickly after you order it.

filthy ADJECTIVE
Something that is **filthy** is very dirty indeed.

First World War PROPER NOUN
The First World War is the war that was fought between 1914 and 1918 in Europe.

franchise COUNTABLE NOUN
If a large company or organization grants a **franchise** to a smaller company, the smaller company is allowed to sell the products of the larger company or participate in an activity controlled by the larger company.
TRANSITIVE VERB
To **franchise** part of a business means to grant someone a franchise to operate it themselves.

franchisee COUNTABLE NOUN
A **franchisee** is a person or group of people who have bought a particular franchise.

fungus (fungi) VARIABLE NOUN
A **fungus** is a plant that has no flowers, leaves, or green colouring. Some **fungi** grow on other plants and have a bad effect on them.

germ COUNTABLE NOUN
A **germ** is a very small organism that causes disease.

horrified ADJECTIVE
If you are **horrified** by something, it makes you feel shock or disgust.

horsepower UNCOUNTABLE NOUN
Horsepower is a unit of power used for measuring how powerful an engine is.

household ADJECTIVE
1 **Household** goods and activities are connected with people's homes and looking after them.
2 Someone or something that is a **household** name or word is very well known.

House of Lords PROPER NOUN
In Britain, **the House of Lords** is the less powerful of the two parts of parliament.

immigrant COUNTABLE NOUN
An **immigrant** is a person who has come to live in a country from another country.

immigrate INTRANSITIVE VERB
If someone **immigrates** to a particular country, they come to live or work in that country, after leaving the country where there were born.

infection VARIABLE NOUN
An **infection** is a disease caused by germs.

innovation VARIABLE NOUN
Innovation is the process of developing new things or products. An **innovation** is a new thing or product that has been developed.

Jew COUNTABLE NOUN
A **Jew** is a person who believes in and practises the religion of Judaism, which is based on the Old Testament of the Bible and the Talmud.

Jewish ADJECTIVE
Jewish means belonging or relating to Jews or to the religion of Judaism, which is based on the Old Testament of the Bible and the Talmud.

Liberal Party PROPER NOUN
In Britain, **the Liberal Party** was a political party which believed in limited controls on industry, the providing of welfare services, and more local government and individual freedom.

luxury UNCOUNTABLE NOUN
Luxury is very great comfort, especially among beautiful and expensive surroundings.
COUNTABLE NOUN
A **luxury** is something expensive which you do not really need but which you enjoy.

market research UNCOUNTABLE NOUN
Market research is the activity of collecting and studying information about what people want, need and buy.

market researcher COUNTABLE NOUN
A **market researcher** is someone who collects and studies information about what people want, need and buy.

Member of Parliament
COUNTABLE NOUN
A **Member of Parliament** is a person who has been elected to represent people in a country's parliament. It is usually abbreviated to **MP**.

memorial COUNTABLE NOUN
A **memorial** is a structure built in order to remind people of a famous person or event.

monopoly COUNTABLE NOUN
A **monopoly** is a company which is the only one that makes a particular product or offers a particular service and which therefore completely controls an industry.

motivate TRANSITIVE VERB
If someone **motivates** you **to** do something, they make you feel determined to do it.

Nazi ADJECTIVE
Nazi is used to refer to Germany from 1933 until 1945, when it was governed by Adolf Hitler and his right-wing political party called the Nazi Party.

nun COUNTABLE NOUN
A **nun** is a member of a female religious community in a convent.

official ADJECTIVE
Official is used to describe things which are done or used by people in authority as part of their job or position.

officially ADVERB
If something happens **officially**, it is approved by the government or by someone else in authority.

over-crowded ADJECTIVE
Over-crowded places have too many people living in them, with the result that conditions are very bad.

palm oil UNCOUNTABLE NOUN
Palm oil is a yellow oil which comes from the fruit of certain palm trees and is used in making soap and sometimes as a fat in cooking.

Pearl Harbor PROPER NOUN
Pearl Harbor is an American naval base in Hawaii. It was attacked by the Japanese in 1941, which resulted in the USA joining the Second World War.

plantation COUNTABLE NOUN
A **plantation** is a large piece of land where crops such as cotton, tea, or sugar are grown.

principle VARIABLE NOUN
Someone's **principles** are the beliefs they have about morally correct ways of behaving.

Prohibition PROPER NOUN
In the USA, **Prohibition** was the period of time between 1919 and 1933 when the law banned the manufacture, sale, and transporting of alcoholic drinks.

protein VARIABLE NOUN
Protein is a substance which the body needs and which is found in meat, eggs and milk.

Protestant ADJECTIVE
Protestant means relating to the branch of the Christian Church which separated from the Catholic Church in the sixteenth century.

province COUNTABLE NOUN
A **province** is a large area of a country which has its own administration.

public company COUNTABLE NOUN
A **public company** is a company whose ownership is divided up into a number of equal parts called shares. It is legally owned by all the people who have bought the shares.

Pure Food and Drug Act
PROPER NOUN
In the USA, **the Pure Food and Drug Act** is a law to control the manufacture and sale of food, making manufacturers say on their labels what is in the food, and making sure that rules on hygiene are obeyed.

Red Cross PROPER NOUN
The **Red Cross** is an international organization that helps people who are suffering, for example as a result of war, floods, or disease.

revolutionize TRANSITIVE VERB
When something **revolutionizes** an activity, it causes great changes in the way it is done.

Second World War PROPER NOUN
The Second World War is the major war that was fought between 1939 and 1945.

self-discipline UNCOUNTABLE NOUN
Self-discipline is the ability to control yourself and to make yourself work hard or behave in a particular way without needing anyone else to tell you what to do.

senator COUNTABLE NOUN
In the USA, a **senator** is a person who has been elected to represent his or her state in the Senate, the more important of the two law-making parliaments.

sheet music UNCOUNTABLE NOUN
Sheet music is music that is printed on sheets of paper without a hard cover.

share COUNTABLE NOUN
The **shares** of a company are the equal parts into which its ownership is divided. People can buy shares in a company as an investment.

silhouette COUNTABLE NOUN
A **silhouette** is the general outline shape of a piece of clothing.

slogan COUNTABLE NOUN
A **slogan** is a short phrase that is easy to remember and is used in advertisements and by political parties.

soda fountain COUNTABLE NOUN
A **soda fountain** is a counter in a drugstore or café where snacks and non-alcoholic drinks are prepared and sold.

stand COUNTABLE NOUN
A **stand** is a small shop or stall outdoors or in a large public area such as a sports stadium.

standardize TRANSITIVE VERB
To **standardize** a set of actions means to make sure that they are always carried out in exactly the same way every time.

starve INTRANSITIVE VERB
To **starve** means to suffer greatly or even die through not having enough food.

stock exchange COUNTABLE NOUN
A **stock exchange** is a place where people buy and sell stocks and shares in companies.

stock market COUNTABLE NOUN
The stock market consists of
the activity of buying stocks and
shares, and the people and
institutions that organize it.

Stock Market Crash PROPER
NOUN
The Stock Market Crash
happened in 1929, when a lot
of companies had financial
problems and had to close, and
a lot of people lost their jobs.

viscount TITLE NOUN, COUNTABLE
NOUN
In Britain, **Viscount** is a title
given to a man by the king or
queen. A **viscount** is above a
baron in rank.

World Exposition COUNTABLE
NOUN
A **World Exposition** is a very
large international exhibition
where many countries have
displays that show their
scientific, technological and
cultural advances. The 1898
World's Columbian Exposition
in Chicago had 27.5 million
visitors and cost $27 million.

Collins
English Readers

ALSO AVAILABLE IN THE AMAZING PEOPLE READERS SERIES:

Level 1

Amazing Leaders
978-0-00-754492-9
William the Conqueror, Saladin, Genghis Khan, Catherine the Great, Abraham Lincoln, Queen Victoria

Amazing Inventors
978-0-00-754494-3
Johannes Gutenberg, Louis Braille, Alexander Graham Bell, Thomas Edison, Guglielmo Marconi, John Logie Baird

Amazing Entrepreneurs and Business People
978-0-00-754501-8
Mayer Rothschild, Cornelius Vanderbilt, Will Kellogg, Elizabeth Arden, Walt Disney, Soichiro Honda

Amazing Women
978-0-00-754493-6
Harriet Tubman, Emmeline Pankhurst, Maria Montessori, Hellen Keller, Nancy Wake, Eva Peron

Amazing Performers
978-0-00-754508-7
Glenn Miller, Perez Prado, Ella Fitzgerald, Luciano Pavarotti, John Lennon

Level 2

Amazing Architects and Artists
978-0-00-754496-7
Leonardo da Vinci, Christopher Wren, Antoni Gaudí, Pablo Picasso, Frida Kahlo

Amazing Composers
978-0-00-754502-5
JS Bach, Wolfgang Mozart, Giuseppe Verdi, Johann Strauss, Pyotr Tchaikovsky, Irving Berlin

Amazing Aviators
978-0-00-754495-0
Joseph-Michel Montgolfier, Louis Blériot, Charles Lindbergh, Amelia Earhart, Amy Johnson

Amazing Mathematicians
978-0-00-754503-2
Galileo Galilei, René Descartes, Isaac Newton, Carl Gauss, Charles Babbage, Ada Lovelace

Amazing Medical People
978-0-00-754509-4
Edward Jenner, Florence Nightingale, Elizabeth Garrett, Carl Jung, Jonas Salk, Christiaan Barnard

Level 3

Amazing Explorers
978-0-00-754497-4
Marco Polo, Ibn Battuta, Christopher Columbus, James Cook, David Livingstone, Yuri Gagarin

Amazing Writers
978-0-00-754498-1
Geoffrey Chaucer, William Shakespeare, Charles Dickens, Victor Hugo, Leo Tolstoy, Rudyard Kipling

Amazing Philanthropists
978-0-00-754504-9
Alfred Nobel, Andrew Carnegie, John Rockefeller, Thomas Barnardo, Henry Wellcome, Madam CJ Walker

Amazing Performers
978-0-00-754505-6
Pablo Casals, Louis Armstrong, Édith Piaf, Frank Sinatra, Maria Callas, Elvis Presley

Amazing Scientists
978-0-00-754510-0
Antoine Lavoisier, Humphry Davy, Gregor Mendel, Louis Pasteur, Charles Darwin, Francis Crick

Level 4

Amazing Thinkers and Humanitarians
978-0-00-754499-8
Confucius, Socrates, Aristotle, William Wilberforce, Karl Marx, Mahatma Gandhi

Amazing Scientists
978-0-00-754500-1
Alessandro Volta, Michael Faraday, Marie Curie, Albert Einstein, Alexander Fleming, Linus Pauling

Amazing Writers
978-0-00-754506-3
Voltaire, Charlotte Brontë, Mark Twain, Jacques Prevert, Ayn Rand, Aleksandr Solzhenitsyn

Amazing Leaders
978-0-00-754507-0
Julius Caesar, Queen Elizabeth I, George Washington, King Louis XVI, Winston Churchill, Che Guevara

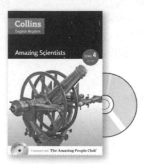